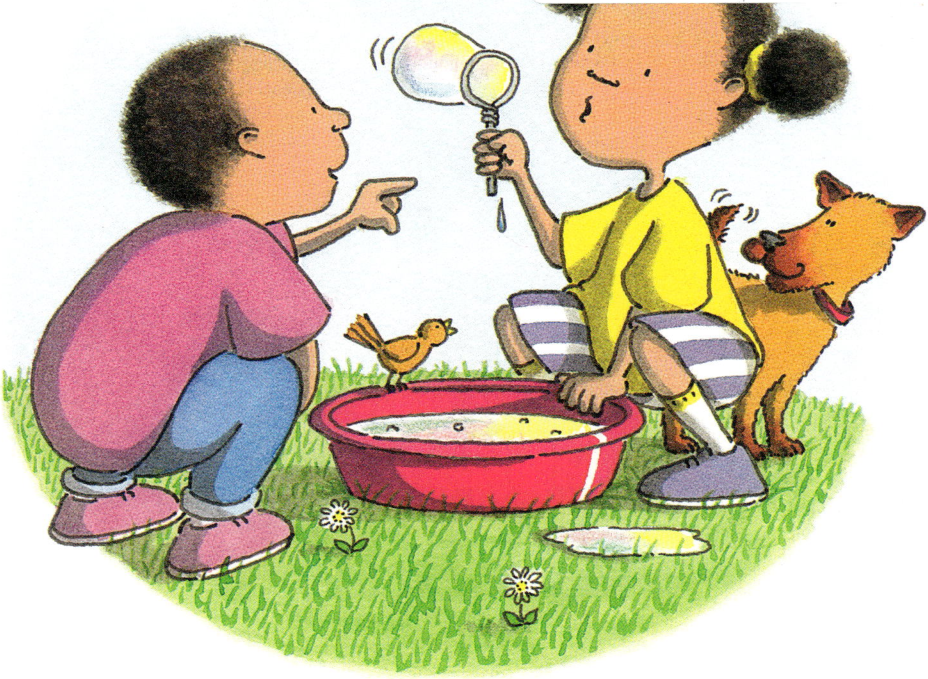

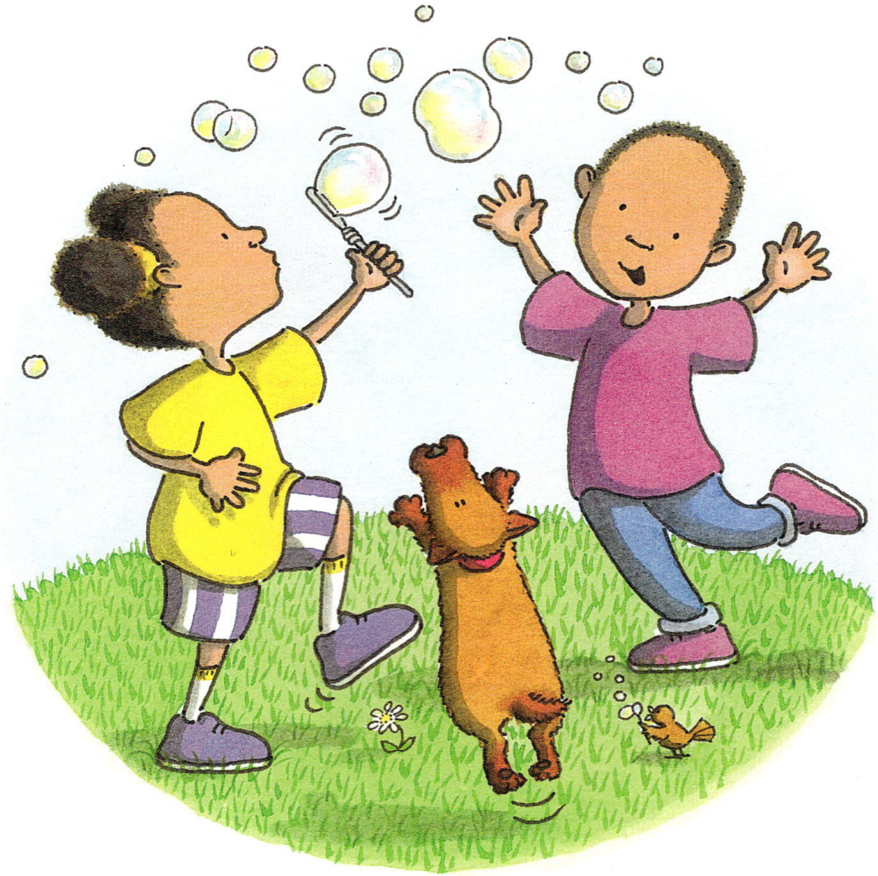

Bubbles in the air.

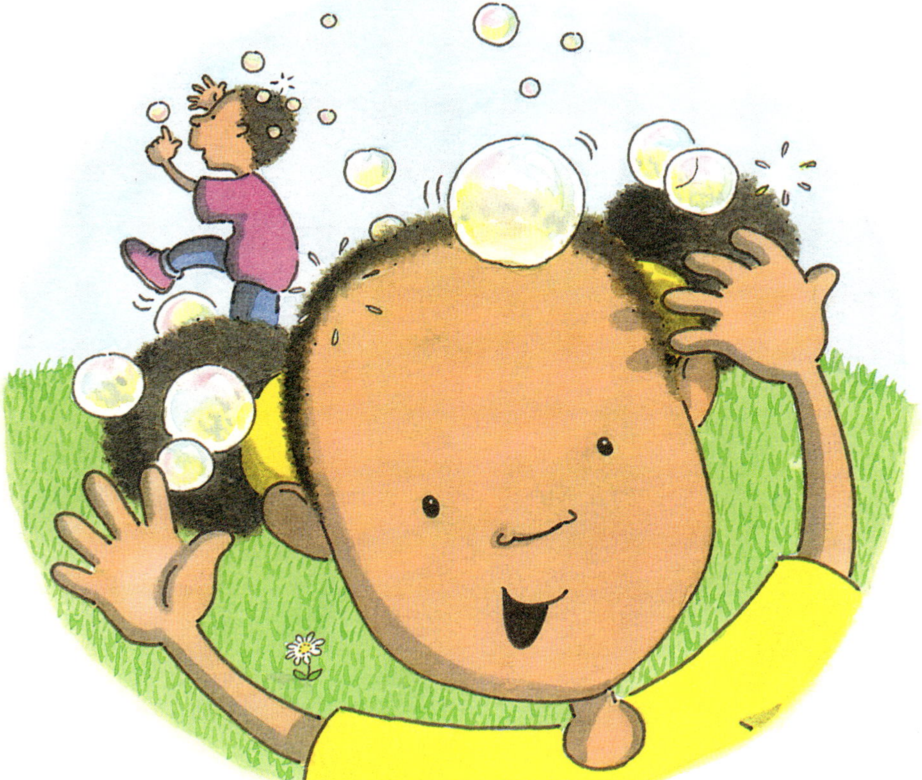

Bubbles in my hair.

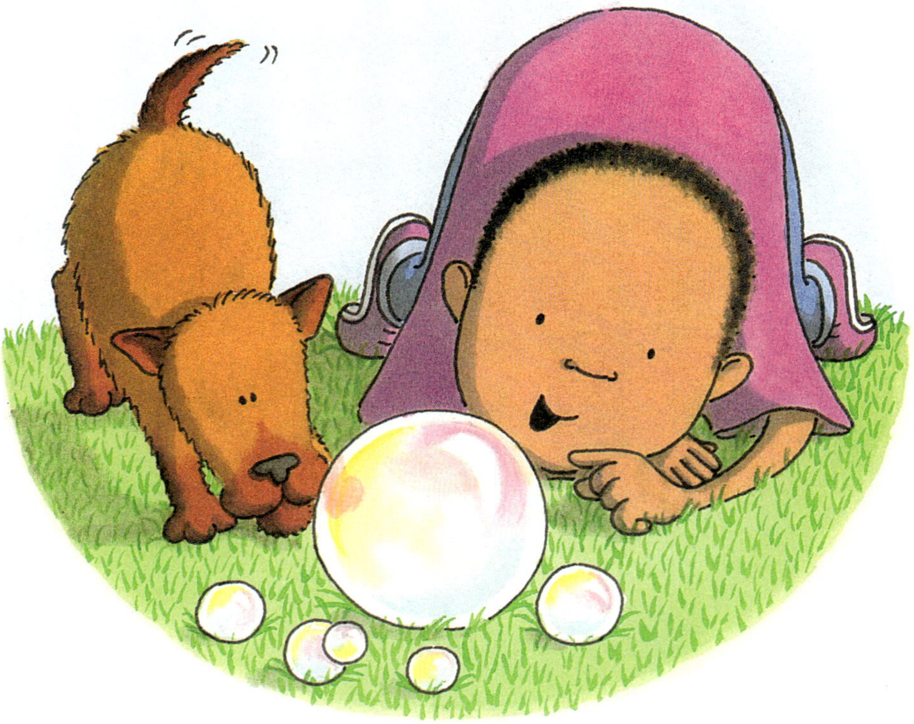

Bubbles on the ground.

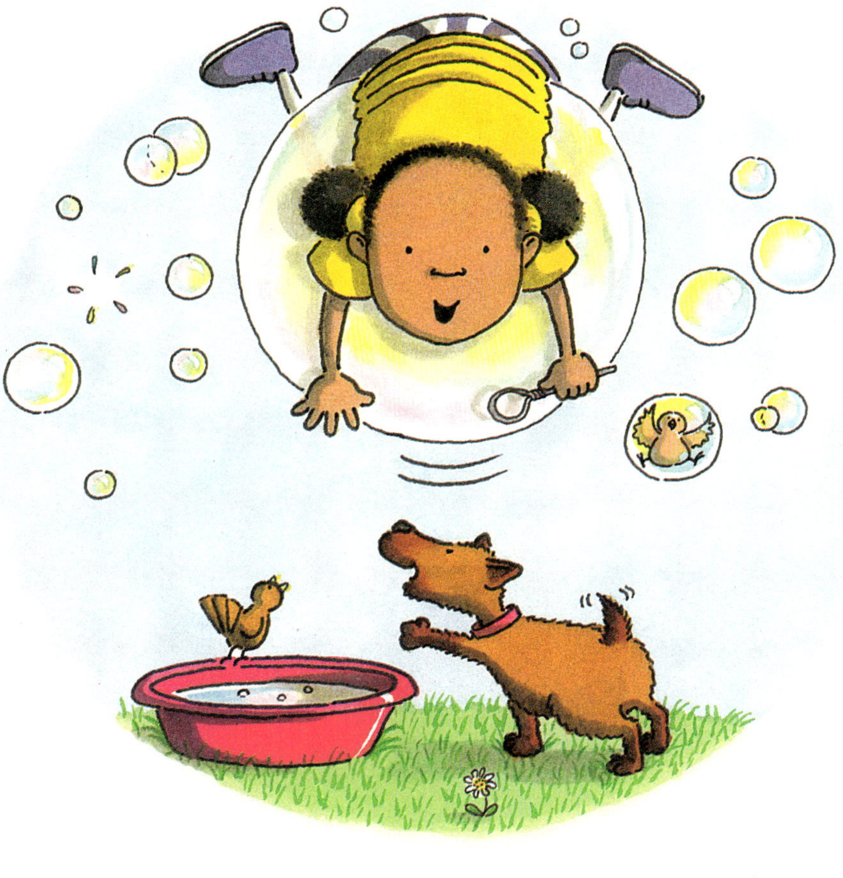

Bubbles big and round.

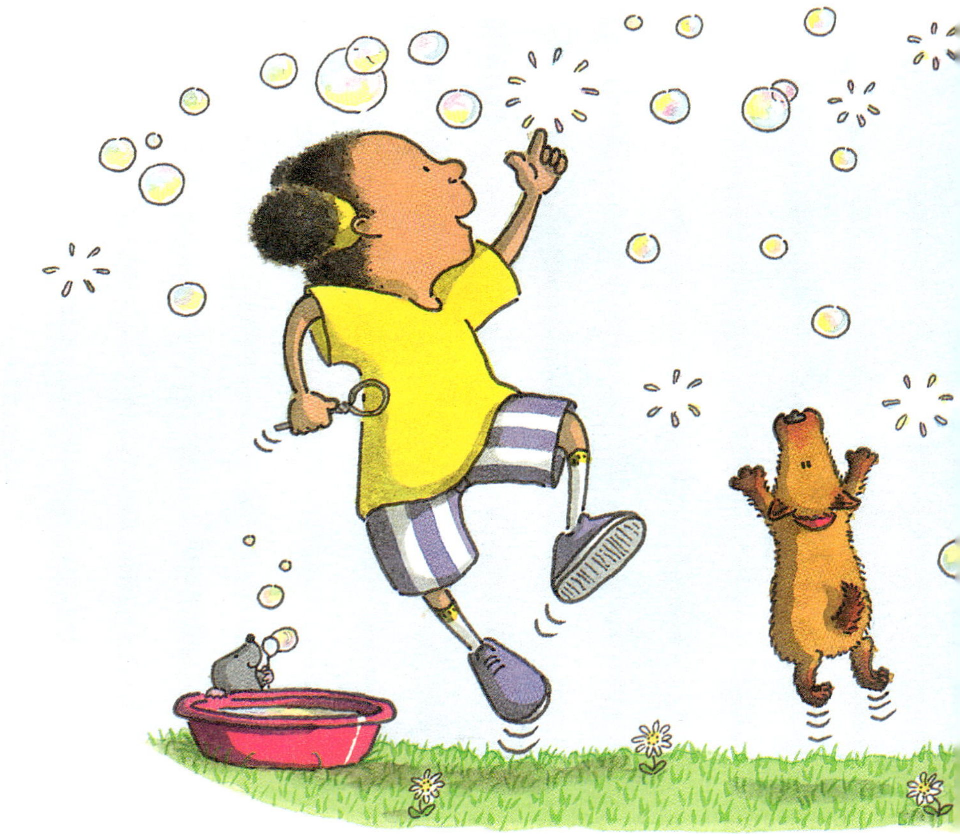

Bubbles bursting high.

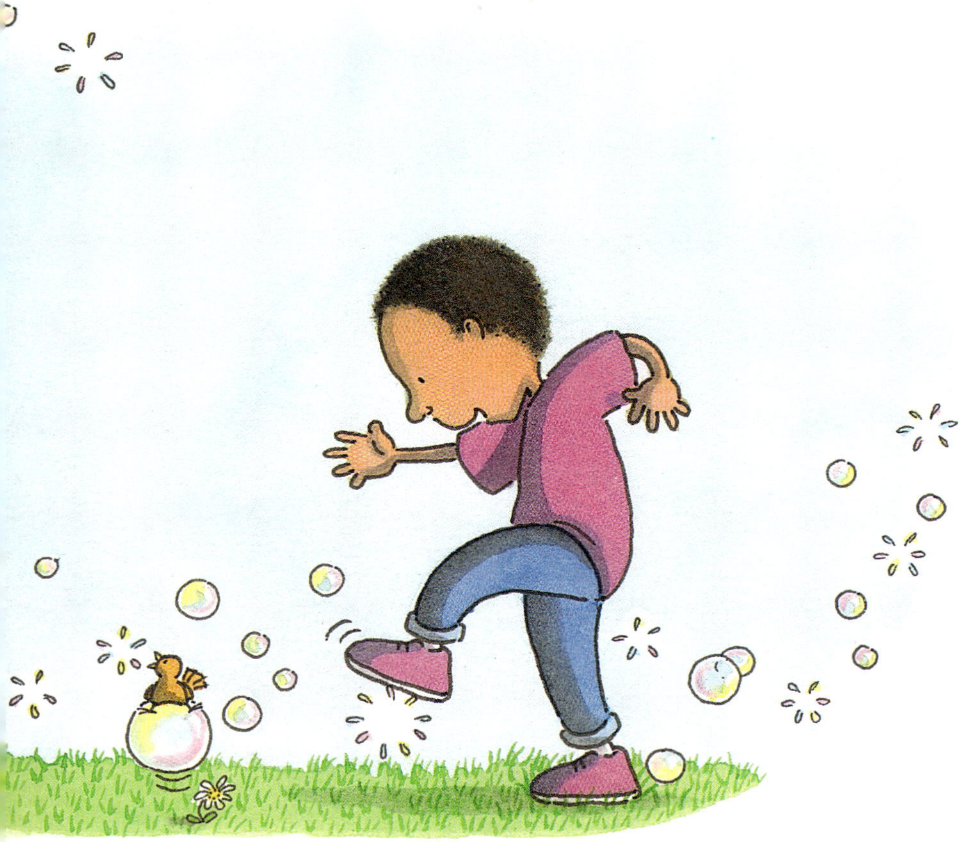

Bubbles bursting low.

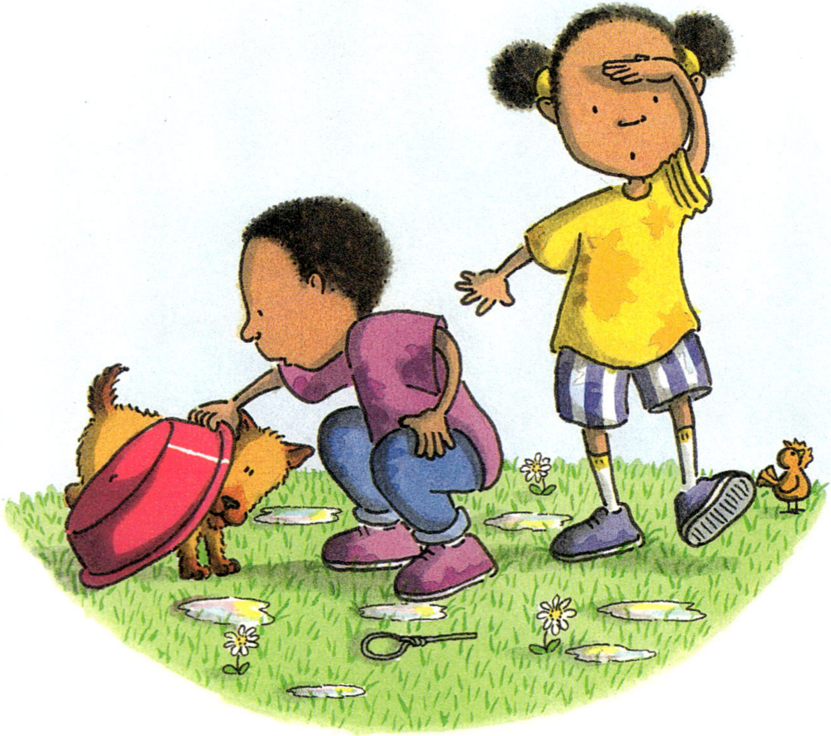

Where *did* all those bubbles go?